ARGENTINA NATIONAL SOCCER TEAMS

ULTIMATE FAN GUIDE

DAVID STABLER

Lerner Publications ◆ Minneapolis

Copyright © 2026 by Lerner Publishing Group, Inc.

All rights reserved. International copyright secured. No part of this book may be reproduced, stored in a retrieval system, or transmitted in any form or by any means—electronic, mechanical, photocopying, recording, or otherwise—without the prior written permission of Lerner Publishing Group, Inc., except for the inclusion of brief quotations in an acknowledged review.

Lerner Publications Company
An imprint of Lerner Publishing Group, Inc.
241 First Avenue North
Minneapolis, MN 55401 USA

For reading levels and more information, look up this title at www.lernerbooks.com.

Main body text set in Aptifer Slab LT Pro.
Typeface provided by Linotype AG.

Editor: Matt Doeden **Designer:** Viet Chu

Library of Congress Cataloging-in-Publication Data

Names: Stabler, David author
Title: Argentina national soccer teams : ultimate fan guide / David Stabler.
Description: Minneapolis, MN : Lerner Publications, [2026] | Series: Lerner sports. World Cup fan guides | Includes bibliographical references and index. | Audience: Ages 9–12 | Audience: Grades 4–6 | Summary: "From Maradona to Messi, Argentina has produced some of the greatest soccer players in history. Learn about the talented men and powerhouse women who make up one of the most successful national soccer teams ever"—Provided by publisher.
Identifiers: LCCN 2025018305 (print) | LCCN 2025018306 (ebook) | ISBN 9798765689363 library binding | ISBN 9798348029289 paperback | ISBN 9798765698549 epub
Subjects: LCSH: Soccer—Argentina—Juvenile literature | Soccer teams—Argentina—Juvenile literature | World Cup (Soccer)—Juvenile literature
Classification: LCC GV944.A7 S73 2026 (print) | LCC GV944.A7 (ebook) | DDC 796.334/6680982—dc23/eng/20250602

LC record available at https://lccn.loc.gov/2025018305
LC ebook record available at https://lccn.loc.gov/2025018306

Manufactured in the United States of America
1-1012734-54804-7/30/2025

TABLE OF CONTENTS

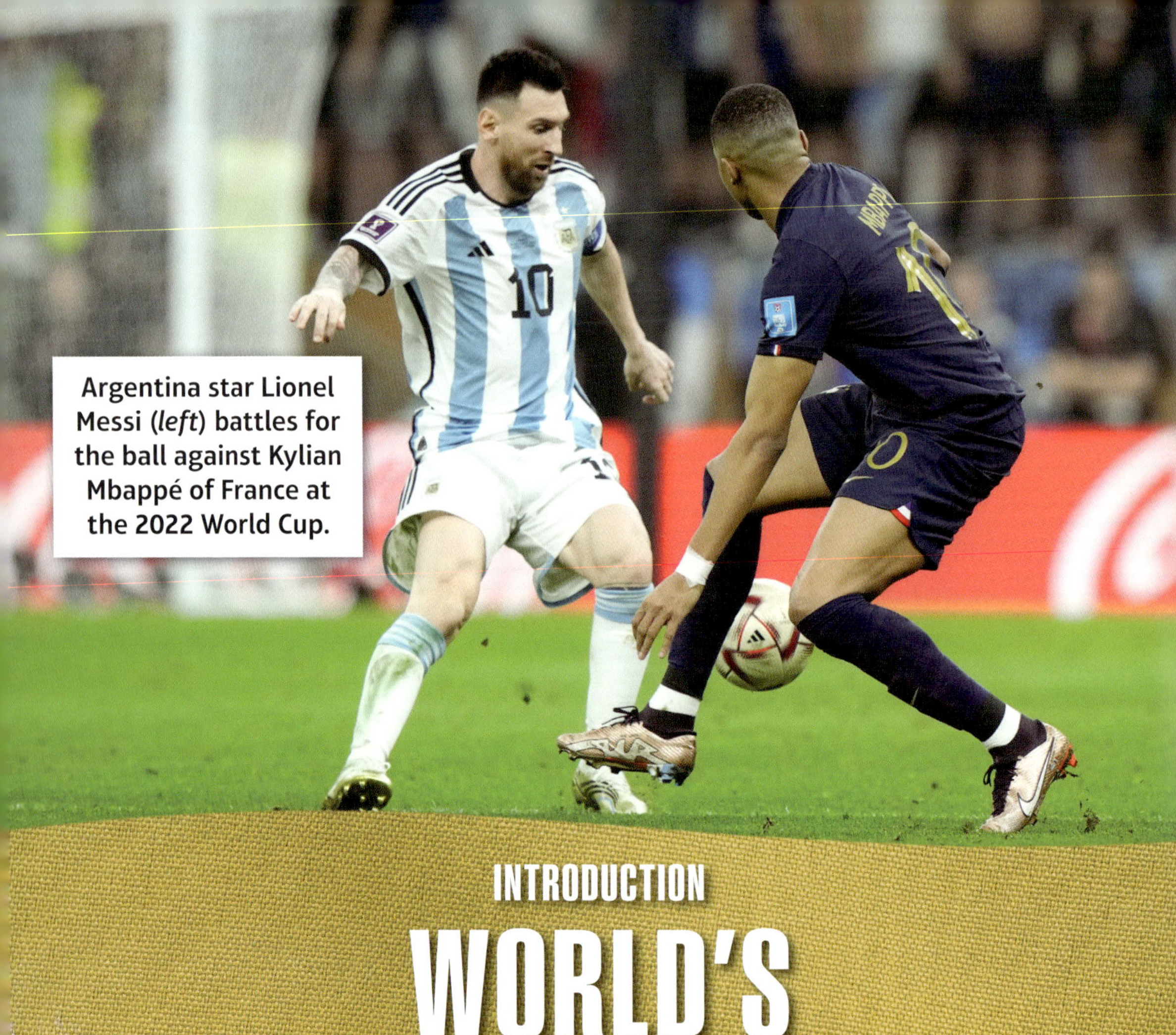
Argentina star Lionel Messi (*left*) battles for the ball against Kylian Mbappé of France at the 2022 World Cup.

INTRODUCTION

WORLD'S FINEST

Fans were on edge during the thrilling 2022 Men's World Cup Final between Argentina and France. The teams were locked in a 3–3 tie at Qatar's Lusail Stadium. The winner would claim the title of best national soccer team in the world.

Lionel Messi, Argentina's star captain, had already scored twice in the game. But France's Kylian Mbappé bested him with a hat trick that tied the match at 3–3. It came down to penalty kicks to decide the contest.

Messi was first. He calmly stepped up and fired a shot. France's goalkeeper dove the wrong way, and the ball hit the back of the net.

Meanwhile, Argentina's goalkeeper Emiliano Martínez was brilliant. He saved shot after shot from the French team. Argentina led 4–2. One more goal would seal the win.

FAST FACTS

Argentina's men's team has appeared in six World Cup Finals. Only Brazil and Germany have appeared in more.

Argentina's women's team made their first World Cup appearance in 2003.

Argentina has played in four Women's World Cups.

The women's soccer league in Argentina became professional in 2019.

Argentina's Gonzalo Montiel stepped forward. He launched the ball to the right side. The French goalkeeper guessed wrong and dove left. Goal! Argentina had won the World Cup!

Argentina goalkeeper Emiliano Martínez makes the save on a penalty kick.

Argentina's Lionel Messi holds the trophy after Argentina's 2022 World Cup final win.

The win marked Argentina's third Men's World Cup title and their first since 1986. It was a huge milestone for the country whose men's and women's national teams represent their country in the World Cup, Olympic, and Copa América tournaments. These competitions each occur every four years, and Argentina makes their mark on every single one. The Argentine national teams pick the country's best players to form winning teams. And each has a long history of success doing it.

Argentina's men's team poses before a 1930 World Cup match. They went on to beat Mexico 6–3.

CHAPTER 1

RISING TO GREATNESS

Soccer is beloved by many of Argentina's people. The country's national teams, both men's and women's, play with great passion and skill. The men's team is considered one of the best in the world, while the women's team is working hard to earn that status.

The Argentina men's team has a long history. It started in 1893, making it one of the oldest national teams in the world. Their first big game was in 1901 against Uruguay. It began a fierce rivalry that continues to this day.

Members of the national team gather in Buenos Aires, Argentina, before leaving for the 1928 Olympic Games.

Another famous rivalry is with Brazil. The teams have had many exciting matches in the Copa América—the South American championship tournament. Argentina also has a rivalry with England because of an infamous 1986 World Cup match.

Diego Maradona is on the attack at the 1986 World Cup.

Mario Kempes takes the ball past a defender in the 1978 World Cup.

Argentina's men's team has played in six World Cup Finals. Only Brazil and Germany have made more. Argentina won it in 1978 with Mario Kempes leading the way. They repeated the feat in 1986 behind Diego Maradona. Then they won again in 2022. The team has also won 16 Copa América championships, showing their strength in South America.

Argentina's women's soccer team has had a more difficult journey. For a long time, women's soccer did not get as much support as the men's game. The team struggled with lack of money, shortage of proper equipment, and poor training conditions. The athletes were even denied locker rooms and had to practice at odd hours. But the team kept fighting for a place in the sport. They played their first big game in 1993 against Chile and won, 3–2.

Argentina's women's team battles the United States in a qualifying match for the 1999 World Cup.

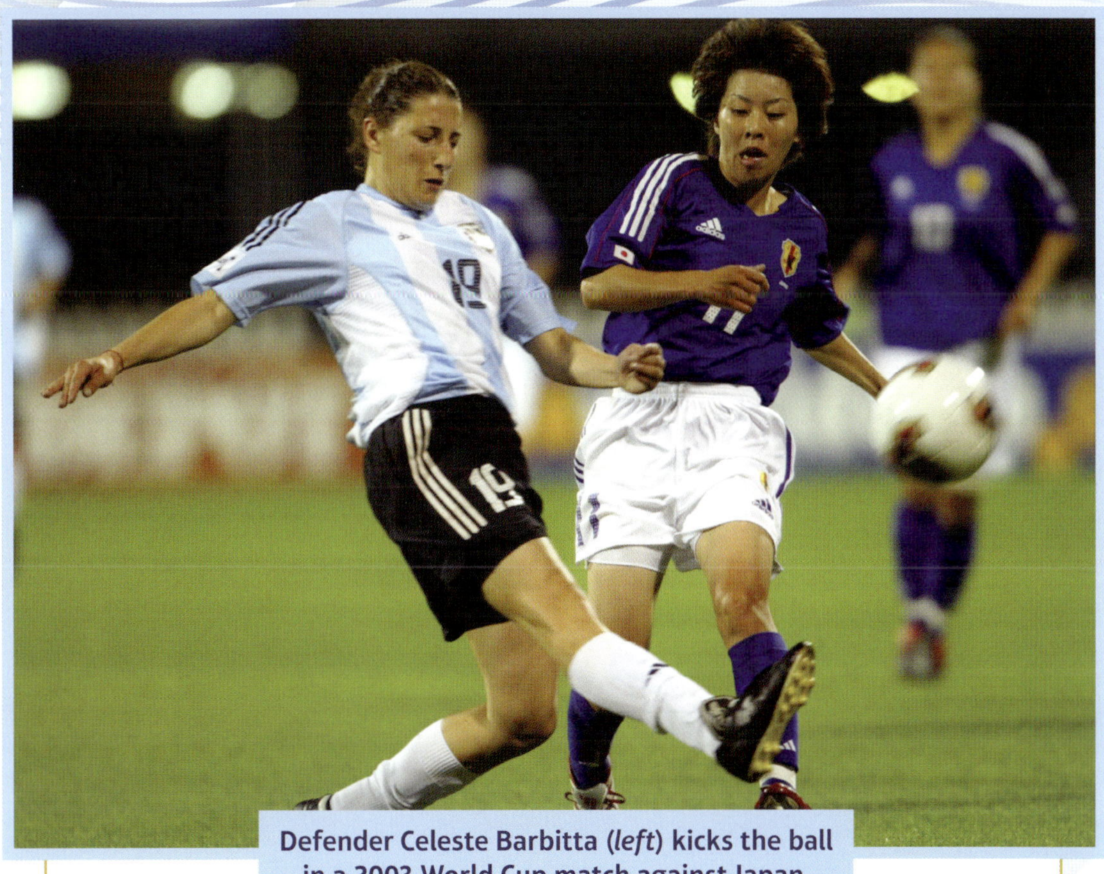

Defender Celeste Barbitta (*left*) kicks the ball in a 2003 World Cup match against Japan.

In 2003, the women's team played in their first World Cup. Since then, they have played in 2007, 2019, and 2023. In 2019, they battled Japan to a 0–0 draw, earning their first World Cup points in group play. That same year, a big change came when Argentina started its first professional women's soccer league. This gave women in Argentina more chances to play and improve. Players such as Estefanía Banini became leaders, speaking up for better conditions and inspiring young girls to take up the sport.

FIRST STRIKE

In 2003, midfielder Yanina Gaitán became the first Argentine woman to score a goal in a World Cup match.

Both Argentina's men's and women's teams show how much the country loves soccer. Their hard work, skill, and passion make Argentina one of the most exciting soccer nations in the world.

Argentina midfielder Florencia Bonsegundo (*left*) tries to get the ball past a diving goalkeeper at the 2019 World Cup.

Argentina players celebrate a goal during a group match against Scotland at the 2019 World Cup.

CHAPTER 2

SUPER MOMENTS

The history of Argentine soccer is filled with exciting moments and great players. The men's and women's teams have both achieved milestones that have made their country proud.

Mario Kempes (*second from left*) scores a big goal against the Netherlands in the 1978 World Cup. Teammate Daniel Bertoni (*left*) celebrates with his arms outstretched.

In 1978, Argentina hosted the World Cup. A powerhouse team led by captain Daniel Passarella and top scorer Mario Kempes beat the Netherlands 3–1 in the final. The fans went wild as they watched their favorite team win soccer's biggest trophy on their own home field.

Argentina won its second World Cup in 1986. One player—Diego Maradona—made it unforgettable.

Known as El Pelusa, or the Fuzz, because of his curly hair, Maradona was a skilled dribbler who could pierce through the opposing defense with ease. In one game against England, Maradona scored two of the most famous goals ever.

Maradona scored the first by punching the ball with his hand. This goal, called the Hand of God goal by reporters, should not have counted. But referees didn't see it clearly, and the goal stood. Maradona then clinched the win by dribbling past five England players to score. It was called the Goal of the Century. Argentina went on to defeat West Germany 3–2 in the final.

Diego Maradona (*center left*) scores his Hand of God goal in 1986. The goal should not have counted, but officials didn't see Maradona use his hand.

LITTLE BIG MAN

Because he is smaller than most of his opponents, 5-foot-7 (1.7 m) Lionel Messi's nickname is La Pulga, or the Flea.

For years, fans thought Lionel Messi would be the next star to lead Argentina to World Cup glory. He set many world records for scoring and was named the world's best player by FIFA eight times. But he could never win a World Cup. In 2022, at the age of 35, he finally did it. Messi scored seven goals and was named the best player of the tournament.

Leading Argentina to the 2022 World Cup title was the crowning achievement of Lionel Messi's great career.

Belén Potassa (*center*) battles for control in a 2007 World Cup match against Germany.

Argentina's women's team has also made its share of history. One of Argentina's greatest games came in the 2006 Copa América final against Brazil. In a stunning upset, Argentina defeated their rivals 2–0 to claim their first Copa América title. Goals from Eva González and Belén Potassa secured the victory, sending Argentina to the World Cup the next year.

Estefanía Banini dribbles the ball in a 2023 World Cup match.

Estefanía Banini stands out as one of Argentina's all-time greats. Fans compare her to Messi because of her dribbling and passing skills. Banini was the captain of the women's team during the 2019 World Cup. One of the most memorable moments came against Scotland. Argentina trailed 3–0, but scored three goals in the final twenty minutes to earn a draw.

Other notable women's players include striker Soledad Jaimes and goalkeeper Vanina Correa. Their skills inspire future generations of Argentine athletes.

Striker Soledad Jaimes prepares to kick the ball in a 2019 World Cup match against Japan.

A young Argentina fan waves the country's flag at a qualifying match for the 2026 Men's World Cup.

CHAPTER 3

CULTURE, FANS, AND FUTURE

Argentina loves soccer. It's more than just a game there—it's a way of life. The fans, called hinchas, are some of the loudest and most passionate in the world. Whether cheering for their local teams or the national team, they bring energy, excitement, and lots of noise to every game. They wave banners to support their team. Imagine a sea of blue and white, the colors of Argentina's flag. That's what it looks like in the stands at an Argentine soccer game.

Hinchas love to sing and chant. One of their most famous songs is "¡Vamos Argentina!" ("Go Argentina!"). When the crowd chants, the whole stadium shakes with excitement. It's like a big party where everyone is celebrating soccer.

The fans don't just sing. They also jump, clap, and dance. They create a wave of movement that goes around the stadium. It's called la ola, like a wave in the ocean.

Argentina fans in white and blue cheer on their team during a qualifying match for the 2026 World Cup.

Argentina fans pack the stadium for a match against Brazil.

Sometimes fans light flares, making the stadium glow. Or they throw confetti in the air. Drums and trumpets play while the fans jump and dance. They do this for club teams, such as Boca Juniors and River Plate, and for the national team. No matter where the game is played, Argentina's fans make their presence known.

WHAT'S A HINCHA?

Hincha **is a Spanish term that translates to "fan" or "supporter" in English. The hinchas often sing in support of their teams. Their songs include the anthem "Muchachos," which honors Diego Maradona and Lionel Messi.**

Soccer is a way of life for many people in Argentina. Here, two young boys practice their skills on the field.

With their World Cup wins and Copa América success, the Argentina men's team is famous throughout the world. Kids across Argentina dream of becoming the next Lionel Messi or Diego Maradona. Young players are stepping up, hoping to follow in the footsteps of their idols. The team has many talented players hoping to become the next big stars. Luka Romero and Alejandro Garnacho are two of the young players ready to lead the team into the future.

Women's soccer is also growing in Argentina. More and more young girls are playing the sport. The women's soccer league has teams from different parts of Argentina. The most successful team is Boca Juniors. The women's national team is also improving, thanks to better support and training. More girls are dreaming of representing their country in the World Cup and Olympics. Samantha Weiss, Yamila Rodriguez,

Samantha Weiss (*left*) fights for control in a 2024 match against Germany.

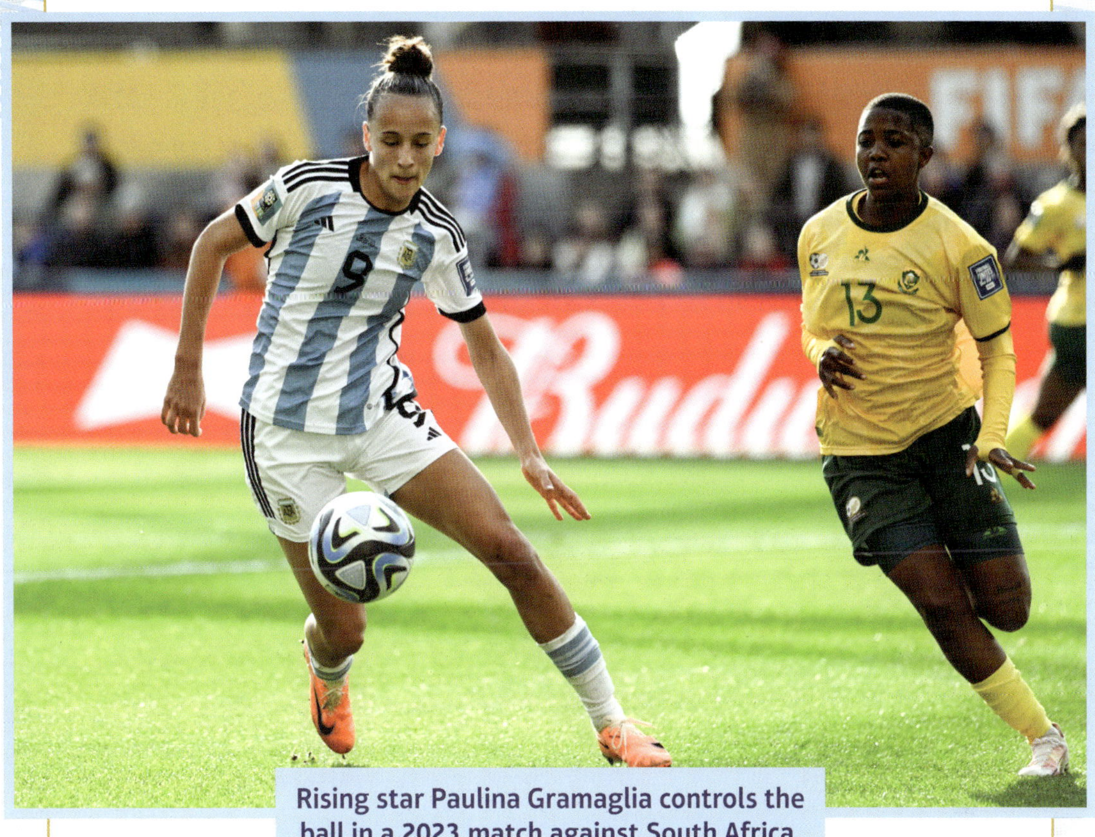

Rising star Paulina Gramaglia controls the ball in a 2023 match against South Africa.

and Paulina Gramaglia are three players to watch as the Argentine women gear up for the next round of international play.

Soccer brings people together in Argentina. It's more than just a game. It's part of their culture. No matter which team they root for, one thing is for sure: the hinchas will be there, singing, chanting, and cheering them on every step of the way. "¡Vamos Argentina!" will ring out for years to come.

ARGENTINA MEN'S SOCCER TIMELINE

1901 Argentina plays its first international match against Uruguay.

1930 The team reaches the final of the first-ever FIFA World Cup.

1978 Argentina wins its first FIFA World Cup, defeating the Netherlands in the final.

1986 Argentina wins its second FIFA World Cup, defeating West Germany in the final.

1991 The team wins the Copa América for the 13th time.

1993 Argentina wins its 14th Copa America.

2021 Argentina wins its 15th Copa América.

2022 The team wins its third FIFA World Cup, defeating France in the final.

2024 Argentina wins its 16th Copa América.

ARGENTINA WOMEN'S SOCCER TIMELINE

1993 Argentina plays its first official international match.

2003 Argentina qualifies for its first Women's World Cup.

2006 Argentina wins its first Copa América.

2007 Argentina competes in its second Women's World Cup.

2019 Argentina qualifies for the Women's World Cup for the first time in 12 years.

Argentina earns its first-ever points in a Women's World Cup.

2022 Argentina finishes third in the Copa América.

2023 Argentina competes in its fourth Women's World Cup.

GLOSSARY

captain: a player who is the official leader of a team

dribbler: a player who moves the soccer ball up the field using their feet

FIFA: a group that oversees international soccer

goalkeeper: the player who stands in front of the goal and tries to stop the other team from scoring

hat trick: when a player scores three goals in one game

midfielder: a player who operates primarily in the middle of the field

penalty kick: a free kick at the goal allowed for certain fouls or to decide the winner of some games

rivalry: a fierce competition between two teams

striker: an attacking player whose primary role is to score goals

LEARN MORE

Britannica Kids: Diego Maradona
https://kids.britannica.com/students/article/Diego-Maradona/490102

Buckley, James, Jr. *Who Is Lionel Messi?* Penguin Workshop, 2024.

Kiddle: Football Facts for Kids
https://kids.kiddle.co/Football

Kiddle: Football in Argentina Facts for Kids
https://kids.kiddle.co/Football_in_Argentina

Scheff, Matt. *The World Cup: Soccer's Greatest Tournament*. Lerner Publications, 2021.

Streeter, Anthony. *World Cup All-Time Greats*. Press Box, 2025.

INDEX

PHOTO ACKNOWLEDGMENTS

Image credits: AP Photo/Jose Breton/Pics Action/NurPhoto, p. 4; AP Photo/Robert Michael/picture-alliance/dpa, p. 6; AP Photo/Martin Meissner, p. 7; Bob Thomas/Popperfoto/Getty Images, p. 8; Haynes Archive/Popperfoto/Getty Images, p. 9; Jean-Yves Ruszniewski/TempSport/Corbis/VCG/Getty Images, p. 10; Action Plus Sports Images/Alamy, p. 11; MediaNews Group/The Mercury News/Getty Images, p. 12; Andy Lyons/Getty Images, p. 13; Julien Mattia/NurPhoto/Getty Images, p. 14; Marcio Machado/Getty Images, p. 15; Dom Slike/Alamy, p. 16; Bob Thomas Sports Photography /Getty Images, p. 17; AP Photo/Jose Breton/Pics Action/NurPhoto, p. 18; Paul Gilham/Getty Images, p. 19; Joe Allison - FIFA/FIFA/Getty Images, p. 20; Eric Verhoeven/Soccrates/Getty Images, p. 21; AP Photo//Gustavo Garello, p. 22; AP Photo/Matias Baglietto/NurPhoto, p. 23; AP Photo/Richard Callis/Sports Press Photo/SPP/Sipa USA, p. 24; golero/Getty Images, p. 25; AP Photo/Andrew Cornaga, p. 27; uda Mendes - FIFA/FIFA/Getty Images, p. 28. Design element: Ralf Hiemisch/Getty Images; Rifqyhsn Design/Getty Images; cunfek/Getty Images; poo worawit/Getty Images.

Cover: AP Photo/Roberto Tuero /SOPA Images/Sipa USA; AP Photo/Kim Price/Cal Sport.